Economics of a Personal Injury Case - Damages and Injuries

Alex R. Hernandez, Jr., Esq.

ISBN: 978-1-941645-52-9

Designed and Published by:

Speakeasy Publications

73-03 Bell Blvd., #10
Oakland Gardens, NY 11364

888-225-8594

www.SpeakeasyMarketingInc.com

DISCLAIMER

This publication is intended to be informational only. No legal advice is being given, and no attorney-client relationship is intended to be created by reading this material. If you are facing legal issues, whether criminal or civil, seek professional legal counsel to get your questions answered.

The Law Offices of Alex R. Hernandez, Jr. PLLC

802 N. Carancahua, Suite 2100
Corpus Christi, Texas 78401

(361) 235-4111

www.PersonalInjuryTrialLaw.org

TESTIMONIALS

I have known Alex R. Hernandez Jr. for almost 14 years. He's not only a great attorney, but also a good friend. He always offers great advice. He's super smart in many areas of the law. He takes great passion in helping people. When he fights, he fights to win! Through the years of knowing Alex, I have hired him for numerous occasions -- for my business ventures, my son in a car accident, legal matters involving an 18 wheeler, and numerous personal injury cases. He represented some of my friends as well. I highly recommend Alex R. Hernandez, Jr. in any legal or business matter. He's also very friendly and trustworthy. He takes great pride in his reputation and his practice. He is the best!!

- Margie

Where can I start; I have known Attorney Alex Hernandez since 2005. I have had the pleasure to have him represent me on many, many occasions. He represented me when my daughter was killed and helped me receive a good sum of money. And then again in 06, he surprised me when we went up against Speedy Stop. He won again. I hired him for a couple of DUI (not on me) and he did extremely well. One was just a fine and he had them drop several other charges. He is dependable and honest and just a phone call away, day or night. Once he was ready to use his personal belongs to help out. He has given advice and helped go up against my city. I have recommended Attorney Alex Hernandez to my family and friends and they have hired him with very good results. If he cannot help you, he will be honest to tell you before taking your case. From divorce, family violence, child support, DUI, personal injury, declarations, he is your guy. It is hard to say what case he handles from arbitration to social security.

- Elva H.

TABLE OF CONTENTS

Author Introduction 7

Misconceptions And Misunderstandings People Have About Personal Injury Claims 9

Claims Process In A Personal Injury Case 13

Why Is It Important To Seek And Follow Medical Treatment? 18

Factors That Need To Be Considered In Determining A Settlement 22

Factors That Can Affect The Settlement Process 25

Factors That Can Affect The Settlement Value Of A Claim 29

Factors That Can Affect The Value Of Your Personal Injury Settlement 33

Costs That Are Recovered In A Personal Injury Settlement 38

Why Is It Important To Contact A Personal Injury Attorney? 41

Author Introduction

For over 15 years, Attorney Alex R. Hernandez has been helping the people of Texas through his skill and effectiveness in law. He is an acclaimed trial attorney who has dedicated his career to passionately and successfully protecting the rights of people in his community. He makes it his goal to represent each client as he would his own family, with hard work, perseverance, and focus.

Alex has been widely recognized for his legal abilities, even obtaining membership in the Million Dollar Advocates Forum, a select group of lawyers making up less than 1% of attorneys nationwide. He also has been top-rated by AVVO, with a rating of 10.0-Superb, and is a member of the Texas Trial Association, an invitation-only association.

Attorney Hernandez and his firm are fully bi-lingual in Spanish and English.

As the son of a renowned Calhoun County judge, Alex was familiarized with Texas law from birth. He received his Bachelor's degree in Economics from the University of Texas at Austin, then went on to receive his Juris Doctorate from St. Mary's Law in San Antonio. In addition, Alex studied International Law at the University of Houston Law Center in Mexico City and has built substantial expertise in real estate law, as well as oil and gas law in Texas.

Alex Hernandez has served on many philanthropic and community boards in Texas including educational boards and food banks. He now also sponsors numerous charities in his Texas communities.

He has the following bar enrollments, certifications, memberships and awards: Texas Bar 2001, Southern District of Texas, Western District of Texas, Certificate in International Law – University of Houston Law Center, Texas Trial Lawyers Association, Million Dollar Advocates Forum Member, and Rated Superb 10 by Avvo.com.

Misconceptions And Misunderstandings People Have About Personal Injury Claims

Most people don't understand that the personal injury process is a very complicated matter. There is the factor of dealing with the insurance companies every single day and handling different parts of the claim including using your own personal insurance or some sort of Medicare or government assistance. All of this becomes very complicated and convoluted.

A lot of people don't understand that you have to pay your personal insurance back. There is an automatic right to subrogation for the insurance companies; it's a right of subrogation for Medicare.

For example, if someone's personal insurance has already paid $8,000 worth of medical bills before he or she meets with an attorney, that attorney will then have to let him know that money has to be paid back.

A lot of clients don't understand that that subrogation claim is a legal claim that the insurance company has against their personal insurance. If you make a liability claim that money gets paid out first. That $8,000 that they took has to either be negotiated down or paid back to the insurance company.

That's pretty important to be aware of. Using our earlier example, let's say the settlement offer is only $10,000. Out of that figure, the $8,000 has to be paid back to the insurance so there is really only $2,000 left to pay the injured person and an attorney.

In meeting with your attorney, he will first ask about your injuries and whether or not you have insurance and whether the insurance is paid or not. Your attorney is going try to maximize the settlement offer.

Challenges Faced During The Recovery Process

Patience is really the biggest challenge faced during the personal injury recovery process. Clients want to know that they are going to get money as soon as possible. However, the attorneys have to know what the injuries are

first. If you have an injury that you've been treating for months, a number can't just be pulled out of a hat.

That's not how it works. The attorney will have to find out the extent of your injuries and how long your injuries are going to last. Is it going to be the next six months? Is it going to be the next two years? Or is this a condition that requires lifelong care? An attorney will help put a value on the injury.

If it's a condition that will last a lifetime, the attorney will have to evaluate the injury with a medical professional. They will ask how long it will take for the injured person to recover and then will go back to the insurance company and say, "The doctor says that it is going to be a lifetime injury and my client is never going to recover."

Value of a person's case

People need to understand that it is not a magical number pulled out of a hat by the attorney. It's based on the factors of the injury, the medical records and the medical bills. The clients need to understand that it is a highly complex process and it's not going to take overnight and it's not going to be tomorrow. It may take several months to get to a point where the attorney will be saying, "We have all your medical records. We have all your medical bills. Now we are going to send them to the insurance company and this is how much we're going to ask for."

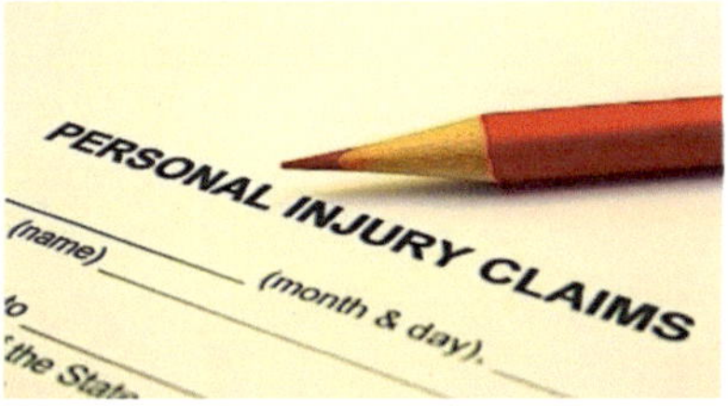

All of this is a process. It's very procedural and it involves negotiating with the insurance company. If they don't pay it, then it comes down to sitting with the clients and saying, "Okay. The next step is filing a lawsuit".

How Long Does It Take To Resolve Personal Injury Cases That Don't Go To Trial?

Everything is on a case by case basis. If somebody has a soft tissue injury and their only complaint is their neck or their back and there is no surgery recommendation, you're probably looking at about six months to resolve a personal injury case without going to trial. It may be the injured person receives treatment for six weeks, and when they're done, they want to go ahead and just close out the case because they feel better.

So again, everything is a case by case basis. You really have to look at the extent of the injury and damages to the vehicle. No case is exactly the same.

Steps To Be Taken If You've Been Injured And Suspect You Need To File A Claim Or A Lawsuit

It depends on whether or not you have an acute injury or a real injury. An acute injury means you've been hit. You go to the emergency room by ambulance and now let's see how fast you recover. In case of a real injury, you've already done all that. You are out of the hospital and you're now taking your medications to ease pain and you are not getting any better.

That real injury prolongs the recovery process. You then need to say to yourself, "Okay, I need to go speak with an attorney to see what else I can do and find out if further treatment is needed."

Many people come in a month later because they had whiplash. As long as they've been treating during that month, and there hasn't been improvement, there might be some issues with recovery.

Overall, it is going to depend on the type of injury and how long that recovery process is going to take.

Mistakes That Could Hurt Injury Claims

One big mistake people make in a personal injury case, is trying to handle it on their own. Once they start talking to the insurance company and their statement is recorded, anything

that was said can't be used in the court of law. However, it can be used against that person in negotiations.

For example, if the insurance company records a person's statement after the accident and they say, "I'm feeling fine. My neck doesn't hurt. I'm just worried about my vehicle getting fixed." Then a day later, that person feels all of the pain from the accident. The problem now is the insurance company has already taken a recorded statement and they will say, "Well, didn't you tell us that you're okay? Didn't you tell us that you weren't really hurt?"

The client may try to backpedal and say, "Well, I only said that because I was asked that the day after the accident. I didn't really know that I was hurt." They are ultimately going to use that against the injured person.

Factors That Make Up A Sound And Viable Personal Injury Claim

When determining what make for a viable personal injury claim, you need to first look at the liability, who caused the accident. If injuries are present and they are clear, you look at the injury of the case. Therefore, if liability is clear and the injury is clear, then the insurance companies will generally make an offer of settlement.

Is Filing A Personal Injury Claim A Relatively Easy Process?

When filing a personal injury claim most people should likely expect it is going to be a fight against the insurance company. A lot of people try to do it on their own, thinking they can handle it. However, once you get on the phone and start talking to the insurance company, it turns out they really are not on your side. They have they are looking out for their own interests.

When somebody that's injured tries to call the insurance company to set up the claim, they'll do whatever "trickery" they can. This includes taking your initial recorded statement and then later trying to use that statement against you.

Handling a personal injury case on your own is really not something that's advised. You need an experienced attorney to walk you through the process.

Do Most Personal Injury Cases Reach A Settlement Before Trial?

Around 90% of personal injury cases are settled before going to trial or before a lawsuit is filed. The 10% of cases that do end up in litigation are typically those with serious issues, such as a

liability dispute or an injury dispute. In larger cases with more serious injuries, there is sometimes a dispute on whether certain major medical treatments are really necessary. Nine times out of ten, however, a case will settle before it goes to court.

Is Going To Court Expensive? Can You Expect To Get A Larger Settlement?

In some cases, you have to get into litigation in order to get the insurance company to really bring any money to settle. Typically, if you file the lawsuit, you're looking at the initial final fees. If you try to do depositions, you're looking at every deposition cost as well.

Once you get into litigation other additional costs will be the attorney's time as it becomes more expensive to interview witnesses and obtain all medical records. You're looking at about $20,000 of costs when you actually file a lawsuit.

When deciding whether or not to file a lawsuit, you have to look at the costs and the risk versus the return. So overall, it does get expensive to file a lawsuit.

Why Is It Important To Seek And Follow Medical Treatment?

Consequences Of Waiting Too Long For Medical Treatment

If you wait too long to seek medical treatment after an accident, you are not going to get recovery from the insurance company. The insurance company only look at a treatment that's been done in the past. If the accident happened two weeks ago, that may be fine. However, waiting four weeks is stretching it and six weeks is too long for most insurance companies to actually pay out or take that into serious consideration.

Most insurance companies use computer programs they input dates into and if the date is not there, then they issue a no recovery letter and they won't give you payment on your injury.

If you have an accident where you needed to see a doctor, then you must to see the doctor immediately. In the event you have been offered an ambulance, make sure they check you over and ensure that you do not have any serious injuries. A lot of the time, when you are in an accident, adrenaline is flowing and you don't realize you were actually hurt. Senses and nerves are affected by the actual accident. You may not know you have a hurt neck or back until the next day or when you go to work out. In most cases, it's not until a day or two after an accident before it actually feels like you were in an accident.

Why Is It Important To Follow The Recommended Doctor's Treatment Plan?

Not following the doctor's treatment plan can have a huge impact on your personal injury case. If you are not complying by what the doctor is telling you to do, then you're not following a

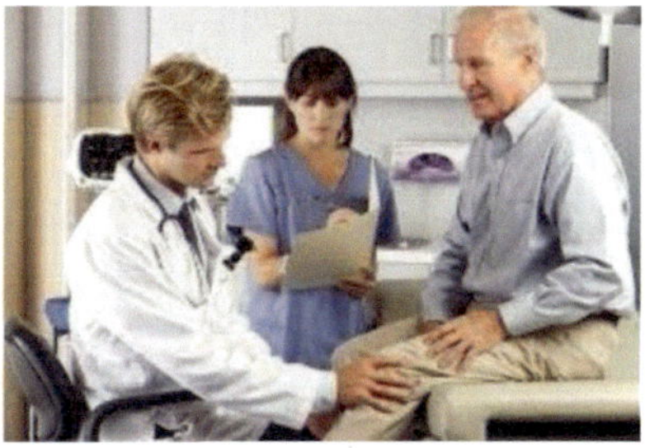

doctor's recommended order. They may mark on your medical report that, "The client didn't come in and did not follow through on recommended treatment." When the insurance company sees something like this they will assume since you were not serious about following medical treatment then you must not be seriously hurt.

There are factors in life that you can't avoid such as work, family and those like matters. However, following the doctor's orders is incredibly important as far as trying to maximize the return you will get from the insurance company.

What Are Gaps In Care And How Will They Affect Outcome Of A Claim?

A gap in care is very important to a personal injury case. The insurance company is looking for consistency; consistency from the time of the accident, to the time medical care was received and then the follow through with that care. They are looking to make sure there are no gaps of time in that care. If there is inconsistency, they may stop payment at a time that you last saw the doctor. The insurance company can refuse to pay after that time, saying that you must not have been seriously injured if the medical care was not followed through on.

Is It An Injured Person's Responsibility To Minimize The Cost Of Their Medical Care?

Someone injured in an accident does not have the duty to minimize the cost of their medical care received. However, the insurance companies would probably beg to differ. A plaintiff's lawyer is not in the business to try to fake an injury or have their client undergo an unnecessary surgery. Usually, you leave all the medical issues to the plaintiff and whether or not they and their doctor have decided what necessity to a treatment is. Someone is not expected to shop around for the least expensive medical care or skip treatments in order to minimize the total costs to the insurance company.

Factors That Need To Be Considered In Determining A Settlement

Components Considered In Determining The Amount Of A Settlement Award

The settlement amount is first of all, based on the liability; who hit the plaintiff, how badly they were hurt. Obviously, a drunk driving defendant or a texting and driving defendant is going to

be held more culpable because of their standard of responsibility than someone who was perhaps didn't act recklessly or have an intent to cause harm.

Next you have to look what type of injury has occurred. If the injury is a of the soft tissue, there will usually be a few months of treatment such as physical therapy or a chiropractor and then they are done.

Then there are the serious injuries that are above and beyond where there may be a six month treatment or longer. You may also have a case where on the date of the accident, you were taken by ambulance or were sent out of town because you had an injury that the local hospital couldn't handle. Those types of injuries can be more expensive and therefore, your recovery is going to cost more. Therefore, your medical bills also play an important part of your injury settlement.

Other Issues That Might Affect The Damages That Can Be Recovered

Whether the accident was a fender-bender or if it was a total loss, the damage to the vehicle might be another factor that will affect damages that can be recovered after an accident

For example, if you have a $20,000 car and it has been totaled out, you know that's a big case because right off the bat you will be out that full amount.

Types Of Damages That Someone Can Recover In A Personal Injury Case

There are several different types of damages that can be recovered in a personal injury claim in Texas. You may be able to recover lost wages, medical bills and pain and suffering. You can also get into bad faith as far as the insurance companies go and talk about treble damages or prompt payment of claims. If the insurance company doesn't properly pay the

claim that you submitted, you can explore what is called "Stowers Demand".

However, as mentioned the main recovery is for lost wages, reasonable and necessary medical bills and then any pain and suffering. In case you have a gross negligence claim, you can actually ask for punitive damages as well. An example of punitive damages might be where an 18-wheeler whose driver has been working beyond what regulations allow and that driver causes a serious accident. Those types of damages not really fixed like the medical records damages.

You also have your bystander damages. Let's say your wife had to take care of you during the time that you were injured, so she now has a loss of consortium claim.

However, the best advice is to call an attorney and see what type of damages would apply to your circumstances and that you could potentially recover.

Factors That Can Affect The Settlement Process

Factors That Help You Decide When Should You Settle The Case

The factors that help deciding when it is time to settle the case can vary. Let's say the case is six months down the line and the plaintiff has done everything he or she could, there is no immediate injury and no future treatment is needed it's now time make that determination with your counsel.

The attorney may say, "This is what the insurance company has offered. Should we take it? This is what the value is." The attorney and plaintiff have to sit down at this point and make a legal determination of whether or not that's a viable amount or offer of settlement.

Again, it's case by case situation. The client's recovery is of utmost importance, and whether he or she is satisfied with what the insurance company has offered is ultimately up to him or her.

Factors That Would Lead You To File A Lawsuit Instead Of Settling The Claim

A lot of determinations on whether or not to accept a settlement are pretty easy. For example, if you have $10,000 of medical treatment and the insurance company is saying, "Well, we give you $500", that becomes easy on whether to file a lawsuit or not. If you have $10,000 in medical care and the insurance company says, "Well, we're going to offer $10,000 of settlement," that's when it becomes tricky.

It then goes into the economics of the case to figure out the risk and cost benefit and what's the reward of trying to settle for medicals versus filing a lawsuit.

Do you pay another $20,000 or more in legal costs in trying to get the insurance company to increase that offer of settlement? Will the insurance company really increase the offer just because you file a lawsuit? There is a lot to be reviewed in these situations.

Threat Of Going To Trial Could Lead To A Substantial Settlement

The threat of going to trial could lead to a more substantial settlement offer. The insurance may start asking themselves, “How much were we going to spend on litigating the case?”

If the company decides it is going to cost $50,000 to litigate the case versus $10,000 in meds and another $10,000 to have the case settled, that just saved themselves $30,000 by agreeing to a higher settlement.

That threat has just substantially increased the client's outcome in the case in settling and reduced the amount that's going to cost to defend that lawsuit.

Is There A Chance Of Losing A Larger Settlement If Someone Ends Up Going To Trial Versus Settling Outside The Court?

The Texas climate has substantially changed in favor of companies in personal injury cases and settlement amounts have greatly reduced. It's not necessarily that the threat of filing a lawsuit makes the insurance companies jump up and say, "No, please don't. And we'll give you more money".

They'll look at it from the same economic standpoint and it's just cost benefit reward analysis. They are not going to offer money just because you've been in an accident. You have to show the injury and the damage. You have to show the liability and also show why the insurance companies should promptly pay that amount of settlement.

Not all insurance companies are threatened by lawsuits. They may say, "No. Go ahead and sue us".

There are a lot of premises liability cases where insurance companies are not threatened because the law is on their side. There are different types of law once you go outside of the auto accident realm. You have to look at every case differently.

When talking about auto accidents, just because you file or threaten to file a lawsuit doesn't necessarily mean you're going to get a better settlement. The insurance company may increase the offer just to avoid the cost of litigation. However, they also may not. It has to be worked out and evaluated on both sides - the plaintiff's side as well as the defense side. You really have to think about how much you are willing to spend filing a lawsuit and the defense has to consider what costs of litigation will be on their end as well. Hopefully both sides can come to an amicable settlement point.

Factors That Can Affect The Settlement Value Of A Claim

How Will Your Prior Injury Affect The Value Of A Claim?

Prior injuries do affect the value of a claim. If you had a back injury before and now you've sustained another similar injury, there are two ways to look at it. You were already hurt in some way before. Therefore, you were probably going to be injured anyway so the value of the case is going to be lower. The other way of looking at it is that you were injured before so there is a foreseeable risk that you're going to get injured again, so your value should be more.

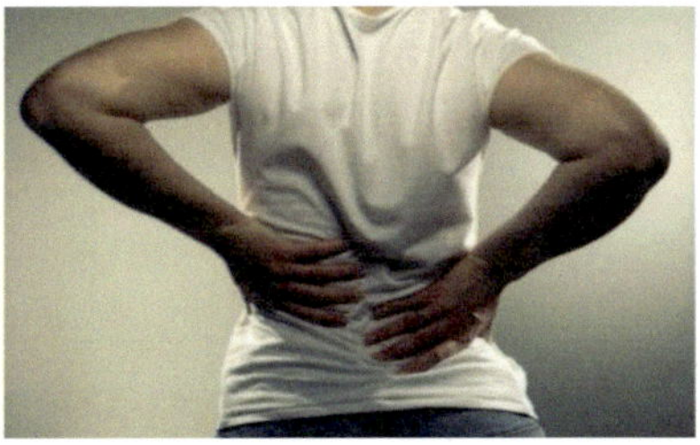

Every case is different as not everybody has the same physical background. If a plaintiff has previously had a back surgery and now needs another after the injury, the insurance and the defense attorney are going to look at it and say, "He didn't get that injury from this accident. He already had the injury." The client's attorney is going to rebut with "The accident has now been exacerbated by this new injury."

So again, there are really two different ways to view preexisting injuries.

Could Someone Recover For An Injury That Aggravates A Pre-existing Condition?

If somebody already had an injury and was recovering and the recovery process is now prolonged by this new injury, it is possible to argue with the insurance company that the original condition has been exacerbated. This would be done through medical doctors and medical experts and through testimony or medical records.

Can An Injured Person Be Found Partially At Fault For An Accident In Texas? How Will That Affect The Value Of The Settlement?

Contributory Negligence or Comparative Responsibility is when someone is partially at fault for the accident that caused their injury. This can actually reduce the amount of their settlement award.

Also, if the plaintiff is found to have been 51% or more at fault, they are not going to receive any kind of recovery because they were more responsible for the accident than the defendant.

What If The Insurance Company Offers A Settlement?

Never take the first settlement an insurance company offers because they may end up offering something more. It is a decision and discussion you need to have with your attorney.

How Are Future Medical Expenses Projected?

Yes, as far as future medical expenses go, it is usually a fair assessment of the doctor's opinion on that matter. If you have an injury and you've been treating and you're not getting any better, you can go back and ask a doctor, "Is the client going to have any more treatment and what the value of that going to be?"

If the doctor then says "He's not getting any better. This is what he's going to require in 10 years", or if he's had a surgery, "He's going to need another surgery in 10 years." A doctor can estimate and figure out how much it's going to cost, what that future medical is going to entail, how long this treatment is going to take and then put a value on it.

Then in 10 years, if you have a client that has a prognosis of future medical and based on today's values, is $100,000 in a surgery, the doctor can say, "Well, in 10 years, based on what's happened in the past 10 years, that surgery is going to cost a $150,000."

Those numbers are important in trying to calculate and get the client to figure out whether or not a settlement should be taken based on future numbers.

If the insurance company does not agree with the future medical costs estimated and says they will not pay it, that's when you have to decide whether or not you're going to let the jury decide whether or not you're going to need that future medical.

Role Of Mediation In A Possible Solution

On the litigation side, every single case has to be mediated before it can go to court. Nine out of ten cases do actually get settled at mediation.

Mediation may cost a couple of thousand dollars for each side to have somebody else listen to the facts of the case and make a determination. The mediator will weigh in on both sides and address any problems he or she sees. Resolving all of the issues in mediation substantially cuts down the cost of litigation. If the meditation doesn't work, the costs of litigation are going to go up and if you're looking at a trial that's going to last two to three weeks versus mediation that lasts two or three days, your costs are cut substantially by the process.

When you mediate, you settle the case and that's it. You don't have to go to trial and spend a lot of time in court and possibly not even win the case.

Mediation is advised in trying to get the case resolved before going into trial.

Do Most Insurance Companies Recoup Funds Once The Case Or Claim Is settled?

The health insurance companies and Medicare will recoup whatever they have liened on. However, if it wasn't for attorneys, the insurance companies would never have recovered those funds anyway.

Therefore the attorney works to try and have the insurance companies reduce the amount to be paid in return because essentially they are getting a recovery of something they may not have ever received had it not been for the attorney.

Insurance companies are the first to be paid back, then attorneys and at the end the client receives the final settlement amount.

Should A Person Protect A Settlement From A Healthcare Provider Or An Insurance Company?

If a person received treatment for anything else such as diabetes or high blood pressure, which was not related to the accident, they cannot include that in the settlement request. However, you wouldn’t go back to the insurance company and say “You don't have to pay us back on that.”

Attorneys protect their clients and make sure that all liens have been paid and ensure anything else that does have is owed is also handled. What does not need to be paid then gets taken out.

How To Collect The Personal Injury Award? How Soon Will You See The Compensation?

The process of collecting a personal injury aware depends on whether the compensation is based on a settlement or if it's based on a jury award. If it's based on settlement, it usually just takes a couple of weeks before the injured party will receive the settlement. Once you settle the case, the insurance company will usually send back a release that you sign and return and soon will receive your check.

You then should hold it in trust and you will start dispersing the amounts to the insurance companies first. Any type of lien has to be paid first versus how it is handled in a jury award. A settlement is easier because you're making an agreement with the insurance company to settle that case. That terminates the case.

A jury award is when you went into litigation and you've won the case in front of a jury. The jury comes back and rewards the amount that you had requested. That's not always the end of it, though. When a jury has awarded you, the attorneys on the other side can still say, "No. We are not going to pay it. We're going to file an appeal."

An appeal can last two to four years and will prolong that award of damages indefinitely. When referring to compensation, there is a big difference between settling the case and making sure that you get the amount versus taking it to litigation. Again, it is a risk where you are taking it before a jury, because you may not get that award.

The insurance company may say, "No, we're going to keep on fighting it till the end. You're never going to see that money. We're going to take it up to the Supreme Court and it's going to last indefinitely."

An attorney may then sit down and talk to his client to discuss whether they want the money now or if they want to go to trial. There is a possible risk that you're not going to win. If you win, the risk is that the insurance company is going to defend it indefinitely. They're going to take it to an appeal, which is going to cost the person another substantial amount of money, especially if they take it to the Supreme Court.

Attorneys are generally paid on a contingent basis. However, if a case goes to trial it may be on an hourly basis and that would be another cost the client is going to have to incur.

A good attorney will try to settle the case so that the client really will get their money, with the only risk being the amount of settlement.

Someone has to keep in mind a jury may not award the amount that they want either. They may aware more or they may aware less. Again, it's a risk. You just have to sit down and look at all the variables and factors that come into either settling the case or taking the case to trial.

Is Payment Typically Made In Lump Sum Or Is It A Monthly Payout?

Many people get annuities because they've been awarded or settled the case for millions of dollars and don't want to take it out in a lump sum because they're afraid they're going to spend it all. In such cases, the attorney can put a life care plan in place and it will be disbursed in payment.

However, if the settlement amount is smaller, such as $30,000, that could be paid out in a lump sum payment.

Costs That Are Recovered In A Personal Injury Settlement

What Are The Non-economic Damages And What's Considered Pain And Suffering?

Pain and suffering is the damage that you feel and is not seen. For example, if you're in pain, you can't say, "Well, that type of pain's value is $100," and so on. You look at it on a case by case basis. If your little finger is still hurting after the accident

versus your knee which has not improved and is and the doctor said you're going to have it for the rest of your life, those are not economic damages that you can see. In other words, you can't put a number on it.

You can't say, "Well, the pain in my hand is worth $5, 000," and "The pain in my neck is worth $20,000." A good attorney will generally ask their client, "What do you think you should get out of this case?"

You can ask somebody and usually for non-economic damages, an expert will be consulted, such as a doctor. The doctor's going to be able to say, "Well, if Client X was not in the accident, this is what Client X would be able to do." How much does is that worth to the reasonable person outside? What is the jury going to think the value is? Those are the non-economic damages that you really can't put a value on or a dollar sign to them. There is no book that says your brain is worth a certain amount or your leg is worth a different amount.

When it comes to pain and suffering, if it is something that you will always have to endure, then that's when you go to the jury and ask for damages.

Minimum Or Maximum Amount That Can Be Recovered In A Personal Injury Settlement

There is no minimum or maximum amount that can be recovered in a personal injury settlement in Texas. You're going to get what your insurance policy agrees to give you.

For example, if you have $100,000 in medical bills and you hit somebody who has $30,000 in insurance, you will only receive the $30,000.

You will only get the amount that matches the policy. You can't go above or beyond that figure unless you want to pursue and what personal assets the person who caused the injury has. A great number of clients, however, usually say, "We don't want to do that. That's what insurance is supposed to cover."

To reiterate, there is no minimum or maximum amount that can be recovered in these cases. The maximum though is sometimes dictated by the amount of insurance.

Why Is It Important To Contact A Personal Injury Attorney?

Do People Think They Can Handle A Personal Injury Case On Their Own?

A lot of people think they can handle a personal injury case on their own. People sometimes think they can look up the information on the internet or that they have enough knowledge to handle things without an attorney. Taking the analogy of doing your divorce; would you ever do your own divorce? If you would, then you're better than a lot of people because know they will probably mess it up.

The same analogy applies to the personal injury case. If you've going to handle it on your own, if you're insurance savvy, then go ahead. Then more power to you. However, it is recommended in either a divorce or personal injury case, to always get an attorney especially if you are only being charged on a contingency fee basis. If you don't recover, then you don't have to pay the attorney.

All personal injury cases at the law firm of Alex Hernandez are on contingency fee basis, so it's up to them to maximize the reward they are going to get for their clients.

Does Hiring An Attorney Result In A Cut In Compensation?

An attorney is always going to maximize the amount of recovery because of his knowledge and experience. Someone can handle it on their own but they are not necessarily savvy enough to understand the pitfalls or the ins and outs of making a personal injury claim and getting the best result possible.

How Can Alex Hernandez Maximize The Value Of A Case?

Being experienced in personal injury, he knows what insurance company is going to do, what they are going to pay out and how he can maximize the benefits for his clients.

Can An Attorney Help To Negotiate Down Medical Bills?

The office of Alex Hernandez can negotiate medical bills on behalf of their client.

What Makes The Law Firm Of Alex Hernandez Particularly Suited In Handling Injury Cases?

The Law Offices of Alex R. Hernandez Jr., PLLC, will take their experience and maximize their client's case based on the value. They can't guarantee results but will zealously represent someone to the best of their ability.

Given Attorney Hernandez's experience in economics, it also allows him to better evaluate the damages of a case, figure out cost benefit analysis and the risk reward. He will value of the case and go back to the insurance company and say, "Okay, this is the value that we put on the case." It is a "pay it or else" kind of philosophy.

His years of experience offer more education to the client, allow more in-depth analysis. He will sit down with a client and utilize his 25 years of experience and apply what he has learned both in economics and in personal injury. Every single case is different. It may be an auto accident, an 18-wheeler accident, or wrongful death case but every single case they take on will be analyzed and defended to the best of their ability.

Made in the USA
Monee, IL
05 November 2026

67386574R00029